MIZZ POETIC TO YOU FROM THE HEART

MIZZ POETIC TO YOU FROM THE HEART

LaVerne W. Henson

authorHOUSE

AuthorHouse™
1663 Liberty Drive
Bloomington, IN 47403
www.authorhouse.com
Phone: 1-800-839-8640

© 2011 by LaVerne W. Henson. All rights reserved.

No part of this book may be reproduced, stored in a retrieval system, or transmitted by any means without the written permission of the author.

First published by AuthorHouse   09/01/2011

ISBN: 978-1-4634-2827-3 (sc)

Printed in the United States of America

Any people depicted in stock imagery provided by Thinkstock are models, and such images are being used for illustrative purposes only.
Certain stock imagery © Thinkstock.

This book is printed on acid-free paper.

Because of the dynamic nature of the Internet, any web addresses or links contained in this book may have changed since publication and may no longer be valid. The views expressed in this work are solely those of the author and do not necessarily reflect the views of the publisher, and the publisher hereby disclaims any responsibility for them.

TABLE OF CONTENTS

DEDICATION vii

ACKNOWLEDGEMENT ix

INTRODUCTION xi

FOREWORD xiii

ABOUT THE AUTHOR xv

WISDOM / ENCOURAGEMENT 1

KNOWLEDGE / UNDERSTANDING 17

THE JOURNEY HOME 29

MARRIAGE 41

BIRTHDAY / THANKS 51

DEDICATION

This book of poems is dedicated to the one that set me apart, open my heart, to hear his voice, to give me a brand new start. He stood by me when I was going astray and needed a friend; he stood by me through all my dark days, troubles and trials. I dedicate this book of poems with all my heart to my Heavenly Father, my friend Jesus, and his precious Holy One.

ACKNOWLEDGEMENT

I would like to thank my daughters Sonia Henson Jackson, LaTonia Henson Gibson, for being patient and listening to all my poems while they were in the making. And a special thanks to Sondra Henson Gilbert, my youngest daughter for typing my Poems before I learned to type. I am grateful to the many friends and co-workers, and even strangers that allowed me the opportunity to write poetry concerning the demise of their loved ones and the revealed truth of their life. I am also grateful to many others who have asked me to write songs, poems, and other situations concerning their personal life.

INTRODUCTION

I am writing this book of Poetry because I believe and have confidence in God that these words of wisdom, comfort and joy, and words of knowledge, will impact the lives of people all over the world. The Lord has blessed me with a talent that only he can create. One day I decided to write a poem for a program, something I did many times before, but never was successful. But this day I starting writing and the words started flowing freely until I finished. It really amazed me. I have been writing every sense. I have learned to rely totally on him for every aspect of my writing. Every thing I have written is related to a true to life situation. I am empathetic toward the people I write about. It is no longer them I'm writing about but its how would I feel if it were me.

FOREWORD

I spent time reading your poems and was encouraged by your diligence in pouring out what God has placed in you. Each one is heartfelt and true. They allow the reader to explore an array of emotions and thoughts. It is wonderful how you have allowed God to use you to open up the lives of others. Continue to let God work through you. Anyone reading your work will be blessed by the wordsmith you possess.

Pastor Anthony Meyers
Youth Pastor
T.D. Jakes/ Potter's House

"We are the voice and the hand that encourages people to change their lives with hope, comfort, and peace."

ABOUT THE AUTHOR

My name is LaVerne Henson; I am a native of Texas. I graduated from the Lincoln High School in June of 1962. I attended the Madam C. J. Walker Beauty College in 1962-1963. I was self employed as a Cosmetologist for several years. I changed my career goals and attended a School of Nursing. After graduating I worked for several years for Hospice at the Visiting Nurse Assoc. Later I united with the Grace of God Baptist Church, Where Pastor R.L.Bonner was the Pastor. This is where my career in writing began. I was the President of the Pastor's Aid, and I tried many times to write a poem for the program, but I was never successful. Then one day I tried and to my surprise the words started flowing and everything started rhyming and in a few minutes I had finished. I was really amazed how quickly the Lord blessed me in writing poetry. My writing is God sent it's a created message in the form of poetry. I rely totally on God for every aspect of my writing. That was the early part of the 90's since then I have written poems of wisdom, words of knowledge, and just plain every day life centered on people, their personal problems and every day situations. I also write songs, and on occasion as the Lord directs I put the words of God to music.

    I am also empathetic toward the people I write about, such as the demise of a family member or friend. The desires of others or any occasion the Lord impress on me to write.

WISDOM / ENCOURAGEMENT

STOP WASTING YOUR TIME

One morning as I was sitting in church, I heard Pastor Bonner say these words, and oh! How they hurt. "Stop Wasting Your Time" I realized my life is coming to an end. Oh! My God forgive me I have sinned. I begin to stop and think how I could make amends, for the time I have left before it's my end.

I considered my ways, my points and views and realized, without the Lord I will lose. I dropped to my knees, I asked the Lord please show me the way, that I may take heed. And now I awake each day leaning on the Lord in every way. He opened my eyes that I may see, wasting my time should not be.

My brother's life could have been saved, if I had done what I had prayed. The battle for a life begins on your knees, but take heed; put feet on your prayers and you will succeed. I remembered the lady with the issue of blood, she had faith in God and believed in His love. She traveled through the city weary and cold, to touch the hem of His garment and be made whole.

Many years ago the Lord said go, witness to Faye, and I said no. I dropped to my knees and said Lord, please, what will I say; and what do I know. Lord you set it up and I will go. To my surprise the Lord is wise. Before I knew it I had a witness too. I looked up and my eyes could see the Lord being baptized as plain as can be.

LaVerne W. Henson

The way you leave this life is not what really matters, but who you know determines where you go. If you know Jesus you will be heaven bound. If not, I pray you get turned around. This life is just like grass it withers as you pass. Stop wasting your time before it's too late, get to know Jesus and your life will be safe.

I have learned my lesson, in sorrow it came. I will start my prayers in Jesus name, then go and witness just the same. Please take heed before you leave, this poem came from the heart, and it's true indeed.

MY PASTOR AND THE WAILING WALL

My Pastor went to the Wailing Wall to pray for us all. He went to pray for every sickness, sin, and whatever the cause, the blood of Jesus cleanses us all. To lie down his cares, yours, theirs, and mine and leave them at the wall. He will pray for Jerusalem here, Jerusalem there, and Jerusalem everywhere.

My Pastor is not a selfish man, he prays for people all over the land. He came to Dallas with a message to deliver, set free, and to heal, come to Jesus while you still have your free will. The door is closing, grace is coming to an end, what will your fate be will you make it in.

The time is now to make your decision, don't procrastinate; tomorrow may be too late. Prayer is being made, time is being spent, come with your love ones with a Y-E-S consent. No one knows the time, or the hour, when the Lord will come in all his power.

Don't be like the five foolish Virgins, but be wise with oil in your lamps, trimmed and burning, waiting for the Lord's returning. My Pastor says prayer empties the heart of its cares. So don't be like the dog that returns to his vomit, give your heart to the Lord and pump your stomach.

When you pray, acknowledge prayer is beyond you, turn it over to the Lord, he made you. Divine directions is received through prayer, take it to the Lord he will get you there. Prayer strengthens your intimacy with the Lord, so call on the Lord to come In-to-You and he will make your dreams and cares come true.

Prayer changes you. So don't manipulate, fall apart, get all out of sort, call on the Lord, he'll give you a brand new start. The Wailing Wall is designed for all to pray. While my Pastor is on his way, lift him up in prayer today. So no harm will come his way. I love my Pastor, His wife, and family too, I thank God for each of you.

BECAUSE

When you have enough opposition, you will learn to get alone with your competition. Trouble will make you pray, so stop trying to hide, it want go away. When God blows a trumpet, the devil's head needs stomping, because he's always trying to make you miss your blessing. God wants you to come up higher and set Satan's Kingdom on fire, with all his imps, cohorts and foes, to take back all your goods he stole.

If you see trouble as a mountain, unreachable, hard to handle, go back to the alter and light another candle, because it takes strong faith; to stand your ground, but if you run the devil will hang around. You have to stand strong and the Lord will never leave you alone. On the other hand, if trouble comes your way and you began to shout and pray and thank the Lord, your breakthrough has come this day, and the devil will get out of your way.

Pastors have come to Dallas, one by one, with a mandate from the Holy One, to lead his people out of bondage, poverty and shame, and tell them to repent of their sins, and be forgiven in Jesus name. However, the going got rough, they said its too tough, we can't do it, the work is too much. My Pastor T. D. Jakes came to Dallas with his wife and family by his side. They moved everything they had, even the cars they drive.

Bishop Jakes mother came to Dallas, his brother and sister came too. God even blessed Mother Jamison while she was at her best, before she went to her rest, to see the beautiful building the Lord has blessed. He not only came with his family, but his friends came too. They left their houses, land and their families too. All to join with the Bishop, with sword in their hand to conquer the enemy and take back our land.

During my Pastor's sorrow, grief and pain as his Mother had brain surgery over and over again. He never stopped ministering to people everywhere, about sin and shame, and the need to be born again. In Deuteronomy:28, you have to read to associate the will of God and man's state. To be obedient is all God asks, and you will reap the benefits and be saved from your past. Bishop Jakes has a mandate from God, to root out, and to pull down, and to destroy and to throw down, to build and to plant, over the Nations, and in every state to build God's Kingdom, no matter what it takes.

My Pastor began to roll up his sleeve, and said, let's fight, I'm going to build God a house; until all the critics are as quiet as a mouse and want to come to the Potter's House. They laughed at my Pastor, because, he didn't have Ushers or Greeters or even Pastors or Leaders. In addition, they laughed because he had to make a new start. And while they laughed, he led his own devotion with a pure heart. David destroyed Goliath with a rag and a rock. Our Pastor is here to serve God with all he's got. If you think you can hold him back, don't be silly, Gods got his back.

    MY GOD, MY GOD, WHAT CAN WE SAY, GOD HAS BLESSED OUR PASTOR IN A MIGHTY WAY.

THE AUDIENCE

Every morning when I awake, I open my eyes to appreciate, my heavenly Father, his Son, and the Holy One. When beginning to pray, and thank the Lord, for a brand new day. He goes before me and paves the way. So there is no one to hinder this day and lead me astray.

I ask the Lord to help me to see things I don't know that hinders me. The answer came, and oh! What a shame, I have to overcome in Jesus name. He showed me this, and he showed me that, but one thing he showed me, is not to look back, but to be bold and strong, face my enemies and hold on.

I was late for Church one Wednesday night and I was led to the corridor on the right. To my surprise, and a great delight, across the hall, stood my Pastor's wife. I froze in my tracks, and could not move; all I could do was wave and be cool. Thoughts came to my head, then I became afraid, to tell her, I wrote a poem concerning Bishop Jakes and the Wailing Wall, her mother, and how the Lord blessed us all.

Help me Lord to overcome this fear, set me free any time this year. Sister Jakes was an audience of one, but to me she represents the Holy One. The enemy did defeat my cause, but I will overcome this great wall, and speak to an audience, large or small, and no fear will hinder my cause.

MAN OF GOD

Man of God let God guard your heart. Don't be hasty, impatient or rude; God is the one to rule. Listen to him, be humble and pray; only God can guide your way. God never grow weary or faint, he never sleeps or turn a deaf ear. He knows your needs and fears. Listen to his call He's the Father of us all. The road is rough; your way is hard, look to the Lord, to give you a new start. Mercy and truth forsake not, nor be wise in your own eyes, trust in the Lord and do good. Walk in the narrow way, and the peace of God will come your way. Stay on the right path and receive your blessing each day.

Man of God the steps of a good man are ordered by the Lord: and he delights in his way. Be meek and humble and always pray. Wisdom and understanding is better than silver and gold and more precious than all the rubies you can unfold. Take all your troubles to the Lord on high your life he will not deny. Many are taking the wide gate as Matthew six and thirteen states, wide is the gate and broad is the way that leads to destruction, the narrow gate leads to life, where you will find the waiting arms of Christ. It's up to you to choose the right path, but whatever the choice good or bad; it's your life so choose right.

Man of God sound wisdom and discretion shall be life unto your soul, honor the Lord with all your substance, and you shall be made whole. Wait on the Lord, and keep his way. The Lord loves judgment, and forsakes not his saints; they are preserved forever, he will never let you faint. Depart from evil, and do good and dwell forever more. He will uphold you in righteousness and guide you from shore to shore. Trust in the Lord, commit your way unto him, rest and wait patiently for him. Cease from anger and forsake wrath. The Lord will find you if you stay on the narrow path.

LaVerne W. Henson

Man of God these words of wisdom come from the heart, take heed to what you read, listen to the Lord; he will supply your needs. When you pray, listen to what you say, ask the Lord to lead and guide you each day. The secret of the Lord is with them that fear him; and he will show them his way. Forever be mindful of God every day, he will be there to point the way.

Henson-7

WOMAN TO WOMAN

Woman To Woman We Are One; Woman To Woman Lets Have Fun. September 11th was a blessing in disguise; it bought us closer together, to make plans to defeat the devil. 2001 we had pain and sorrow, until we learned, God holds tomorrow. This is a New Year 2002; God will bless us this whole year through.

Woman To Woman We Are One; Woman To Woman Lets Pray To The Holy One.
On our way to a new start, let's stay together and never depart. Ministry is our goal, let God take control. After all is said and done because of Gods Son, we have already won.

Woman To Woman We Are One; Woman To Woman Lets Give God Our Little Ones.
Never the less the word of God is sure, we put our trust in him and we are secure. We love our First Lady, she was sent to us from above, Oh! What a wonderful Father to bless us with her love. The word of God is true, when we follow his directions; He will always see us through.

Woman To Woman We Are One; Woman To Woman Let Us Fast To Take Part Of A Great Task.
To be in Gods presence, and be filled with his love, pray, give, and fast, and you will receive from above. Love the brethren, it will be the same, as you fear God and reverence his name. Put your trust in God, he will draw you near, perfect love casts out all fear.

My Dreams for Two Thousand and Three

My Dreams will come true, because every promise of God is directed to me and you.

I am committed to do God's will, lead me, guide me and teach me when to stand still. Stir up my spirit that I may have complete confidence in the things that you ask, so that I may let go of my pass. I want to come up higher, so bless and show me the way, that I may be your servant each and every day.

To meet my husband in two thousand and three and live happily ever after, with the one the Lord has prepared for me

I will have my home in two thousand and three, because the word of God has promised it to me. I can have what I say, just be faithful and pray. <u>May 2006</u>

Thank you Lord for my family. Touch, direct, save, and set free. Don't let them be the same in two thousand and three. You are the Lord the God of all flesh, there is nothing to hard for you. Thank you Lord for bringing my family through.

My new job as a DSO, will bless me so, I will be making more money, than I will ever know. My new job as a DSO, will be mine without a doubt, the Lord has promised, and I'm going to shout!. <u>July 12, 2004</u>

I will publish my Poems in two thousand and three, I know the Lord will bless, His hands is on me. He will open opportunities I can not see, he will finance the gospel for you and me. <u>January 10, 2011</u>

Lord bless my friends that they may be, a blessing to you in their ministry.

And yes Lord, lead me, bless me, and show me how to be a friend, that I may be pleasing to you in the end.

These are my dreams from long ago, they will be answered this year I know. I may not be where I need to be, but I'm not where I was before he saved me. Just like Job, he had to go through pains, and sorrows, not knowing what holds tomorrow. This is my year, two thousand and three, open your eyes and see God's favor is on me.

WORSHIP THE LORD IN ALL THAT YOU DO

Worship the Lord in all that you do, follow his lead, he's talking to you. Continue to be kind hearted and true, with time, focus and dedicated efforts: things will happen for you. To have and to hold is a plan designed for two people to unfold, male and female created he them, to love and to hold a long life, and grow old.

Don't be fainthearted, dismayed and blue, the Lord will be there for you. Stop trying to figure out the things you didn't do, or make things happen because of the way they look to you. Some people are mean, unruly, hateful and just plane rude, but it's not the people with a good or bad attitude, it's the position they hold, to get you to your goal.

We walk in the flesh, but to war in the flesh is not of God. We yield to the Spirit of praise and worship in all that we do causing the Lord to come to your rescue. Jesus loves you weather you are good or bad. Don't give up it will only make him sad. Trust the Lord in all that you do, look to him he will see you through.

Trials come to make you strong. But always remember, God will guide you from his throne. Pursue your journey where the Lord is leading you. Stop worrying about the pass it will only make you sad. Looking back will make you stumble, fall apart or anything but be humble. Remember Lots wife; it hindered her chances to continue in life.

If you want to succeed, worship the Lord and follow his lead, He will supply your every need. Open your heart and mind he will reveal to you the things that made you blind. Knowledge and discernment is what you need. To develop wisdom and judgments just fall on your knees, the Lord will answer, and you will be pleased.

Struggles and trials may bring about pain, but without pain, there is no gain. You only go through things your faith allows you to, so look to the Lord, he's able to see you through. The words of God are Spirit and they are life. They are without strife. So speak God's word with the fruit of your mouth, and God will increase the blessings of your house.

My Pastor said something that meant so much "There are no perfect people, husband, wife, children, or so, what ever you got, if we work it out we can put it in the pot, together we can have a lot." The enemy is losing his grip he has to let you go. If you are looking for someone to give you one hundred per cent, stop looking.

It was Gods Son. He was heaven sent he gave us one hundred per cent. I can give you eighty and that's a lot, I'm only human, what have you got. Weapons of our warfare are not carnal, but mighty through God as we struggle through our troubles. When God pull down our strongholds we see our way clear, thanks are to God we can conquer every fear.

KNOWLEDGE / UNDERSTANDING

DEPART FROM EVIL

Depart from evil and do good, seek the Lord the way you should. Give him honor and glory. Your peace will tell your story. Raise your hand in every land, let them know your God is grand, and you will dwell forever more, to tell of God's glory from shore to shore.

Summary

The Lord dealt with me about writing this poem. I was reading from Psalms 37:27. Soon after he told me to write the poem I had to transfer to another bus, where I met and talked with Chantey. I wrote the poem and Chantey read it and said it was for her, so I gave her a copy. After getting to work Loy, another coworker came into the break room wrapping a song, and I knew in my spirit that this poem was meant for him too. I gave him a copy. As he read it out loud he started wrapping it as thou he wrote it himself. I am thankful the Lord uses me in some small way to tell his people of God's glory and help show them the way.

GOD GAVE ME ANOTHER SISTER

One day many years ago, I prayed for a friend, one that will love me through thick and thin. A friend I can confide in. As the bible states, by love we should serve one another, and thanks to you Lord she is a blessing to me like no other. She is like a little sister, kind hearted and friendly as can be. Thank you Lord for sending her just for me. I am not alone, I have someone to talk to on the phone, and someone to care as we travel here and there.

And bless me Lord to do the same, to love my friend in Jesus name. To be concerned, kind hearted and true, and confide in each other as only you will have us to do. Lord you said in your word, there is a friend that sticks closer than a brother, and you have blessed me with a friend that is as dear to me as a mother. You answered my prayer and Oh! What a day, to have a friend that's so dear in every way. Thank you Lord for sending me a friend today.

As Carol and I was standing side by side, the Lord revealed to me by His spirit in a very special way, she would be my sister this day. It was impressed on my heart as simple as can be, thank you Lord for opening my eyes to see. She reminds me of my sister, you called home that day, thank you Lord, for sending another sister my way. A few years back, as I recall God gave me a dream, and now I know what it means. It came to me, as plain as can be.

I will know who my husband will be. I want have to worry, argue, or fight, I will know him by sight. The same way the Lord revealed to me my sister that night.

GOD'S LOVE TO MAN

Man was made in the likeness of God, with all his love, joy, and intricate parts. Men were made to dwell on earth, just like Jesus did, as he was created in birth. He came to teach and bless us to see all of Gods creation, was intended to be. A life full of love, joy, and peace, that will fill us with his glory, so all the world can see, our master loves you and me, so we can tell (His-Story).

Man came first, to pave the way for his bride on their wedding day. He prepared a place for his bride that day, warm, and full of prayer, just like Jesus did when he made Adam, and set him there. Man was made to till the ground, and keep his bride safe from all harms that are around. He holds her heart in the palm of his hand, because he knows what it takes to be a man. To have and to hold his wife, to love and cherish her as he was told, he realized there is no end to this blissful life that God will not unfold.

THE CLASS OF TWO THIRTY FOUR
DALLAS COUNTY SHERIFF DEPARTMENT

January 10, 2005 to February 4, 2005

We began our class the first month of the year, to set the stage for all that will come here.
We were excited and scared but full of cheer; we all had different goals, and plans for the New Year. We had a variety of teachers for every subject in the book, we had so much to study, I wanted to scream and holler, then I realized that was my problem. My attitude was so bad, it made me sad. I had to go through, because I know God is here to see me through.

The first two days were great, Sgt. Wilson told us we had to tow the line, or get left behind. He's one of a kind, he's patient, diligent, understanding but tough, don't get me wrong you have to do your stuff. Ms. Flannigan is kindhearted, devoted and oh so sweet. She will never let you be negative, she'll keep you on your feet until you are complete, and she's always discrete. Sgt. Presley is such a dear, she will help you, coach you from far or near, on her breaks, during her lunchtime, or whenever she can find the time.

DSO Watson, Sgt. Sellers, Sgt. McKenzie, Mr. Tipton and DSO Cortez, we will remember the things they said, it all contributed to what we need to get ahead. Lt. Sanders, Mr. Sweet, Chief Daberko, Mrs. Kramer and Sgt. Teal they were very informative and real, especially about the gangs, they could get you killed. Mrs. Rogers is very good and particular with her facts, but she want give you no slack. Just like diseases they can be fatal, there is no turning back.

Mizz Poetic to you from the Heart

Sgt. Artesi, Sgt. Lawrence, DTO. Kunjappy, Mrs. Olson and Ms. Pattway and all the others that are not named here today. They were very explicit and kind, thanks to every one for relinquishing your time. Deputy Morning, SRT. Ballard, and Deputy Chavez, they worked us out from head to toe; now we know we have a long way to go. We need self-control, to keep our balance to stay in control. DTO Brooks, Officer Calhoun, Officer Ruiz, Officer Cooper, and DSO Shaw, and all the others that was portraying the

Parts of an outlaw played their parts from their hearts to let us know we had to do our parts. Sgt. Hodge you are the man, that gave us the OC Spray, I believe every classmate would like to shake your hand, and lead you to the promise land. We started out with twenty-six, but some could not stick, but never the less they will always be a part of the class of twenty-six. We set the goal to be continued forever more, always remember the class of two thirty four.

THE GRACE OF GOD

I confess and I believe as I make this statement I will receive. I will be out of debt in ninety three, the Lord will bless, this years for me. My house note, car note, and bills galore, thanks are to God I will have no more.

My decision is made, my prayer has been prayed, my mind is made up, I will stand on Gods word, and I will not give up.
This book of the law shall not depart out of my mouth, I will reframe from speaking vain words, and I will be quiet as a mouse.

I will meditate day and night, that I may observe to do according to all that is written therein, my God is faithful he will see me through in all that I will prepare to do. After I have done all that I have said, the Lord will make my way prosperous, and I will have good success, my God is able to bless.

I will not be afraid of sudden fear, neither of the desolation of the wicked when it cometh; for the Lord shall be my confidence and keep my foot from being taken. So get behind me Satan, before long you will be shaking. After all hope is gone, I will stand on the word of God, because all that he said is in my heart.

TIME IS PRECIOUS

Time is but for a moment, set up for the entire world to see. Time is for all eternity. To fulfill our days before the time of our end is here. Time is precious every waking hour from sun up until sun down time is the working of Gods power.

Time being used wisely, as the ant prepares ahead, so in winter he can sleep and slumber on his bed. Time used like the rabbit, which builds his house on a rock, unlike sand, stubble, or hay that is blown away.

Times are precious; given from God above all humanity covered with his love. Hours, days, months and years add up. All is well under the Masters touch. Time is like the locust, it moves in unity with the body.

Like Dan, Bobbie, Kathie and me we all have different deeds, used to satisfy your needs. Time is like the spider, he uses his web to conquer and defeat, and given a chance, he will make his home in a Palace suit.

Time is precious, to which there is no end. Get to know my Jesus and you can live free from sin. He is the one to hold your hand, so open your heart and let him come in.

LIFE IN THE FAST LANE

Life in the fast lane is merely a game. With two players or many the results end in shame.

Life in the fast lane will always be a disaster. You will never win if the Lord is not your master.

Life in the fast lane is fun, exciting, and full of fame. Life in the fast land is void of Jesus name.

MY SCHOOL WORK

My School work and assignments are almost complete. Thank you Lord for blessing me with all I will need this week. I like my job, my hours are grand, especially when everything goes well as planned. Where I work is a blessing from God, because it's not every where you can study on the job. Finishing school is one of my major goals. Thank you Lord for all the wisdom it holds. My school work will soon be complete, and I will celebrate at the end of the year, with praises and songs and Christmas cheer.

THE JOURNEY HOME

I WANT LET GO

Another day has come and gone, and Homer has preceded me home. My heart is heavy and full of pain, my husband left me all alone to manage on my own. My dreams and plans may be scattered. I may be shaken and full of woe, help me Lord! I want let go.

As I recall, Homer and I had made plans to travel over the land, have fun viewing the sights, or just watching the stars shine at night. No matter the plans or season, spring, summer, winter, or fall, we were goner have fun doing it all.

Life has taught me to quote the word of God. It gives me hope, and helps me to cope. In Isaiah 30:29 learn these words given from our Lord Divine. "When you rise early in the morning with a song and gladness of heart, it will cause Gods glorious voice to speak to your heart."

It is my time to say good bye, your time has come and gone, you are no longer here, and you left me on my own! But I must continue on. I will miss you so, but no! I want let go. I will see you when it's my time to go.

My Grandmother

I visited my Grandmother a few days ago; we laughed and talked, and watched a TV show, then it came time for me to go. I told her goodbye, I would visit her again soon, and I left the room. My Auntie and I were driving back home, and to my surprise, my cell phone rang. They told me my Grandmother is gone; she's no longer in pain. My eyes filled with tears, she was only here for a few years.

I loved my Grandmother, she was like a mother to me, and she was the love of my life. She told me to avoid strife, and let God have control of my life. My heart is heavy, I'm full of grief and all I want to do is holler and scream, and kick the walls with my feet. My Grandmother didn't tell me she was going home and leaving me all alone, I don't know what I'm going to do, and who will I tell my troubles to.

She was full of encouragement, wisdom, and care, what will I do now, she will no longer be there, My Grandmother raised me from when I was a child. She told me to be kind and sweet' and young ladies never walk the streets. But as I recall, my God is the comforter of us all. He left his home in glory' to tell us of His-Story; how he bled and died on Calvary to set every soul free, so we can live in victory.

My Grandmother's life has changed; she's with my God that reigns. So I will make a change, even though it came about with pain. I will rejoice and be happy, fill my spirit with the word, transform my life and continue to live for Christ. Yes! I will cry and be sad, but I will be peaceful and glad. Goodbye my Grandmother, you lived your life holy, as will I, when my time come, I will join you in glory.

MY HUSBAND IS IN PEACE

My Husband is in peace. He left late one night, he was in a hurry to catch his flight, yes we said goodbye, I knew he was going home on high.

Yes! I will miss him sitting in the Den, watching TV, or sitting on the Patio viewing the sights with me.

Cooking his favorite meals, even paying the bills. We were together for many years. And one day he left me with my eyes full of tears.

Now he's gone, but my memory will forever linger on. He is where he's safe, where pain and sorrow has no place.

Goodbye my love, I know you are in peace, walking on the golden streets, where singing and praising the Lore will never cease.

ONE LAST LOOK

One day I passed my mothers room, she called me in, my hand she took, all she said, I only want to look. She did that not just once, but twice you see my mother was trying to say goodbye to me.

She called Michelle and me into her room she tried to tell me then, daughter! I will be leaving soon. I didn't understand, nor did I recall, my mother was trying to say goodbye, she's leaving us all.

On Valentines Day she went away, left all her family and friends she loved, to be with my God above. I stopped by her house, one last look I took, as I recall she'd open the door and grin, as my brother and I would come in.

I talked with my mother just hours before she left, she was clean and fresh, and looked so peaceful as she slept. Now my mother is gone, a long way from home, she is free from sorrow, sickness, and pain, she's with my God that reigns.

A LOVE THAT'S NEVER LOST

I was married when I was just a child. I was self taught, but I always had a smile. I talked a lot to get attention, and people listened to my good intentions. My husband taught me many things about this and that, but now I know better, and I try not to look back. Help me Lord to understand, I need your guidance as I make this stand.

One day I met my sister as I was told, she was sweet and kind to me but she wasn't very old. We had our ups and downs we didn't get alone that well, but oh! How I loved her and every one could tell. My mother kept putting us together, and we would go different places here and there, then one day she moved away and left me standing there.

We kept in touch, down through the years a love that's never lost even the distance can't erase a heart full of joy filled with tears. A few years ago I was told my sister was sick, and that made me sad, because I couldn't go until after some time had passed. My time came to make the trip, I was happy as can be, and she seem to cheer up as soon as she laid her eyes on me.

We talked for hours about things we loved, places we have been, until it was my time to go, oh how I loved her so. She seemed very weak, but she was so sweet, help her Lord to get back on her feet. But at home as time passed on my sister died and left me all alone. She didn't even say goodbye. What can I do now Lord but trust n you, help me Lord to make it through.

The Lord gave me a sister a few years back, we fall out occasionally as sisters do, that's a fact. We will always share that sisterly love from the hand of God above. And as friends we will always be until our time on earth take us to our destiny. Thank you Lord for a love that's never lost, through heartaches and pain, sickness and even shame we look to you Lord to make us whole again.

LaVerne W. Henson

For the love of a sister for such a short time really makes me sad. But! It is better to have loved and lost than never to have loved at all. Help me Lord! You know my heart; I will love you until its my time to depart. Thank you Lord for my sister and the time we spent together, I will cherish them for ever. My cross is my lifeline to happiness and peace. We will meet again when we sit at Jesus feet.

MY LAST HOPE

I lay in bed from sun up till sun down. I wonder what's happening all around. I am useless, I do nothing but complain about pain. My arms hurt, legs hurt, back hurts here, my side hurts there. Lord I'm hurting everywhere. I hurt and complain the whole day through My life is so useless I don't know what to do. I have tried all, spent all, it's nothing they can do. Lord! My last hope is in you.

I surrender my life to you Lord, I repent of all my sins. I ask you to be my Lord and Savior that I may make it in. Time has bought about a change, I will no longer complain, but I will give my life to you Lord, and be thankful just the same. When my days on earth have ended and I close my eyes in sleep, all my pain, sickness and sorrow I will lay at Jesus feet.

THE LOSS OF A SISTER

The Loss of a sister, or whoever it may be, is a void that life will bring to all that be, until the end of eternity. No matter what the circumstances, or how it came about. We will all go someday to meet the master, weather we are large or small, God is the maker of us all.

It's all right to be sad, sigh, or cry, but only for a little while then dry your eyes, pull yourself together, and thank God for the time you had her under your feathers. God is wonderful, kind, loving and strange, he will see you through, just call his name.

He will change your life, and you will never be the same. The loss of a sister will always be just remember Jesus died for you and me, so we can make the change, from death to life and live with Christ. Your destiny is not determined on the day of your death, but from the way you lived your life.

Each step you take determines your fate. Open your heart let Jesus fill you with his love. Listen to the Lord; he will wash you in his blood. As you read in Genesis 4, you will see how Abel believed and obeyed Gods command, and at the end of his days he was safe in Gods hand.

Cain disobeyed God did not keep his command. He was a fugitive and a vagabond and traveled all over the land. The Sabbath was made for man and not man for the Sabbath. The loss of any life is precious in Gods sight. Remember the Sabbath day and keep it holy.

Meditate on Gods word day and night and you will do what is right. Take heed to the words of God; meditate on it long and hard. The time is at hand for you to hold on to Gods hand. The Lord knows your heart. He will never leave you nor forsake you if you keep him in your heart.

SHE WAS ALWAYS THERE

I was sitting in my house, in my favorite chair, not having a care, I looked up and my sister was there. When we were in school, we played by the rules, but we had lots of fun, we played tricks on everyone. We were Twins, we made it hard, no one could tell us a part.

When I go shopping in a mall, on a trip, or a cruse, even when I move, no matter where, my sister was always there. We sang in the Bishop's Choir, she sang alto, I sang soprano, and we praise the Lord, as they played the piano.

My friend and I went to the pool we were really cool. I called my sister on a whim, and she joined us for a swim. On this Good Friday, I find myself without her, she has gone home, she beat me to His throne, but I am not alone, Jesus is here to comfort me, until its my time to go home

I thank you Lord for the time we spent together, she's in a better place, where she will live forever. We were born to die, no matter how we may cry; it's my time to say goodbye.

MARRIAGE

STRANGER AT MY DOOR

One day as I was sitting inside I heard a knock from the outside. I opened the door and to my surprise, there stood a tall dark stranger with a hat on his head and shades on his eyes. I invited him in and with a grin he began. He measured my rooms from the Kitchen to the door, the wall and even the floor. He told me thus and so and what I should know. I said OK, you do the walls and such, leave the floor, it's to much.

My tall dark stranger was friendly to me. I said to myself, maybe this is the way it should be. My tall dark stranger came more and more to my door. I began to look and want him to come even more. I began to wonder and ask God why? I saw one man in a vision across the sky and another from a distance with the same description. My heart began to flick and flutter, I began to wonder, what was the matter?

Back to my knees, Lord! I will pray, guide me to the right guy this day. After a few days my tall dark stranger is reluctant to give his love for me, because of his will. My heart is heavy full of despair, no one to love hold or share. The stranger you sent is full of care. He's also scared and running every where.

He holds my heart in the palm of his hand. Help me Lord, I know that you can. I need you Lord to fill his life with the love of God to make things right. Save his life, fill him with your love, good things come from God above. Thank you Lord for answering my prayer. I will love my stranger with out despair. He will love me, hold me and we will share, that Jesus is the answer to my prayer.

WALKING TOGETHER

Walking through the meadow hand in hand, we share our thoughts as we hold each others hand. The flowers are glowing with all their colors so bright, Oh! I thank the Lord for such a wonderful sight. The trees are standing tall, and they are stout, they look toward heaven as though they want to shout.

We stare at the sky, to make a wish from on high. The sun, the moon and stars, shine from your Son the Holy One. The land is beautiful, filled with his love, made especially for us from God above. As we stroll through the park, it's so peaceful and quiet. We thank you Lord for all the good things you blessed us to acquire.

We have our ups and down, we have had conflicts all around. but you have blessed us to overcome, and now we can conquer each and every one. Each step we take, whatever plans we make, we thank you for your grace. The food we eat, the clothes we wear, all come from your special care.

We lift up our hands, to praise you in the land, and give you thanks, for your Son so grand. For every thing we do, we acquire it through you.

MY HUSBAND TO BE

I have waited down through the years, sad and lonely, sometimes my eyes filled with tears. But I remember good things come to those who wait, no matter how long it takes. My husband to be will soon be with me. Thank you Lord my time has finally come, we will soon be together as one.

The spirit of the Lord leads me to know, if I follow his lead I will not be lacking in what ever I need. This is my year Twenty-Ten a blessed year for my husband to be, to come in. I will not give up. I will meet my husband to be as soon as the Lord sends him to me.

It will be sometime this year. Oh! What a blessing when we come together with a cheer. I never wanted to marry a man that was a Pastor, Evangelist or so. But now I have changed, help me Lord I'm willing to let it go, and except the man you prepared for me that I may grow.

Lord you said write the vision and make it plain, this is it Lord you hold the reins. Just like you took Eve from Adams rib. I want to be the rib of my mate you will bless me to meet, so we can marry and our life will be complete. I desire to have a man of God, with integrity.

I want to marry a man that's powerful, loving, and true, one that will love me, and especially you Lord and put you first in all that he do. Help me Lord I will be patient, and wait for your directions, so I can meet the right guy and have no doubts or questions.

TO HAVE AND TO HOLD

My life is grand, no matter how I stand. The Lord has blessed me on every hand. My family is well as can be, my home so lovely and sweet, my car I drive with all that power at my feet. I go here and there, I do as I please; but now I know, I'm missing something I really need. Save me Lord, set me free, so I may live with you in eternity.

As I kneel and pray I adore you Lord in every way. Forgive me of all my sins; help me Lord to make it in. Your word says if I confess with my mouth the Lord Jesus and shall believe in my heart that God has raised Him from the dead I would be saved. Lord! I believe and I confess, thank you Lord for your righteousness.

Jesus paid the price for all humanity that day on the cross, and because of you I am no longer lost. No matter how I stand, I know my God is grand. He will grant my petition for my mate to be, because He said no man should be alone, and that includes me. But Oh to have a mate from day to day to have and to hold, what my life would be like as it unfolds.

To walk hand in hand, to go different places would be so grand, to hold my mates hand. No matter how I stand, I put the Lord first in all my plans. You said to write the vision and make it plain, so Lord hear it is, I desire my mate to be a man of integrity, good, courageous, loving, and kind, just for me. A man that prays and loves you dearly, and loves me with all his heart sincerely.

Thank you Lord for answering my prayer. We will meet one day because I know you care, and one day soon we will be on our honeymoon.

TO BE

I will meet my husband one day soon, It may be from a glance across a room, or around the corner on the street, across the sea, or on a beach: may be in a church, or in a crowded room, however we meet, one day soon, we will be on our honeymoon.

In proverbs eighteen and twenty-two every word of God is true. My husband is a man of God, kind, loving, and wise, looking for his bride to stand by his side. I love the Lord with all my heart, no man will ever take, God's part of my heart.

I have been divorced for many years, engaged twice; but departed in tears. My time has come, and is now, not all the hours, days and years of my pass will compare with the long wait at last. No matter who he may be Lord, whenever you send him through, we will have a wonderful life, all because of you.

IF I HAD MY WAY

If I had my way I would choose you this day, but I would live without fulfilling my destiny in every way. You are sweet, kind, loving and strange, all you have to do is change, give your life to the Lord, and start over again.

If I had my way, and would yield to my flesh, my life would be miserable, because there would be no happiness. I have been married once, engaged twice; never again will I choose a Spouse, unless the Lord bless his house, and tell me he will be my Spouse.

If I had my way I would be out of control, so I'm listening to the Lord, and will do as I'm told. My destiny is in God's hand, and I'm willing and obedient to do his command.

If I had my way, and you were in Christ, I would choose you too be my husband, and I would be your wife. I have made the choice, to live my life in Christ, and let the Lord, send my mate, and not choose in haste, but wait for my mate.

I FELL IN LOVE WITH YOU

By: Quiuna Jackson

There are no words I could convey, the adoration I feel for you in every way. There is no way I could ever dream for something as powerful and true, as all the love I have for you.

I live for your smile I dream for your kiss when I am with you it is pure bliss. One look at your face gets me weak in my knees don't say good-bye I beg of you please.

You are my life I am your girl I feel so special being in your world.

So hold me tight and before you let go there's just one thing I think you should know. With one look in your eyes I knew it was true with the touch of our hands I fell in love with you.

TOGETHER FOREVER

Today is our wedding day, a new beginning for Paul and me. To stand at the altar hand in hand, to be at peace with God and man. To say our vowels, before the crowds. Thank you Lord you have made us proud.

We will work our plans and pursue our goals, and let God take control, as we walk down the threshold and our lives together unfold. A new adventure to become one, and pleasing in the eyes of God, the Holy One.

To make our plans for all to see, God has blessed Paul and me, to live together forever. We thank each and every one of you, for being a part of our great start. From the tallest to the smallest, for our gifts large or small. If only a thought, we appreciate you all.

BIRTHDAY / THANKS

THANKS FOR ALL YOU HAVE DONE

My new car will be a blessing soon. I choose to have an Infinity from the Car's show room. My plans are grand for my new car in Two Thousand and Ten. Thank you Lord for all you have done, you made my life enjoyable and fun.

You open doors I could not see, you made everything as plain as can be. My life has changed from disaster and more, thank you Lord for opening every door.

Thank you Lord for the Auto Pound, my first job after three years of being out and around. Thank you Lord for my first apartment after one month of employment, what can I say, you made it happen that way. Nine months later in December two thousand, I drove My Ninety Six Mitsubishi on a cold day home in the snow, what a way to go.

After a while, I had to let my apartment go. Working at the Auto Pound I didn't make that much money you know. Then I moved to Altoona and I had to move again sooner. My third move was OK. I stayed there until the Lord made a way from Westmoreland to where I am today.

Thank you Lord for my new job as a DSO, and all the money that come with it in Two Thousand and Four. And my home so sweet, it's a wonderful blessing you have given to me. Two Thousand and Six represent man, thank you Lord you have blessed me with all this land.

My husband to be is a man of integrity. He's bold, strong, courageous, kind hearted and sweet. Thank you Lord for a wonderful mate you will bless me to meet. It may be on a beautiful night or day of the 27th, or what ever date it may be it will be ordained from heaven.

STARTING OVER

This is a new day, a new beginning, I am asking you Lord to forgive me of my sin. I will praise you forever more, I will be thankful for you opening every door. Thank you Lord for all you have done. My life will no longer be a disaster, because today you are my master. My life has been saved because Jesus died and came back from the grave. You gave me my life, my family and friends, thank you Lord; I know you will bring them in.

I need you Lord in my life, to lead and guide me and keep me from strife. Now that I have a new life, I need a friend, a companion for life. To meet my husband one day soon, my life will no longer be in gloom. I will praise you Lord for evermore. We will be happy and rejoice as we travel from shore to shore. Thank you Lord for preparing my husband to be only for me, so we can love each other and forever be free.

You said in your word Lord, whosoever finds a wife finds a good thing and obtain favor of the Lord. I am praising and thanking you in advance for my soon to be mate. We will have good romance and happiness because you blessed us to relate. I will have a husband soon and we will be on our honeymoon. He will be committed Lord to your will and ways. He will be bold, courageous, and strong, oh! What a love I will for ever hold on.

MY ANSWERED PRAYER

Thank you Lord I have received double for my trouble.

This is the year the Lord has picked, to bless me with my home in Two Thousand and Six. Thank you Lord for my new home so cozy and sweet, and all my furniture inside will make it complete. My address of thirty-three-ten tell the story of a blessed end.

    The first three-represent the three days the Lord laid in the grave. And rose the third day and made death behave.
    The second three-represent the thirty-three years Jesus walked on earth to teach and train us of his only Sons birth.
    The one represent the Trinity, The Father, The Son, and The Holy Ghost, Three in one. The Divine Father, Blessed Son, and The Holy One.
    The zero-represent lack, famine, void of money and fame, but none of this matter if you have faith in the Father and pray in Jesus name. Your blessings will come and you will be sustained.

Thank you Lord for my Living room furniture you will bless me to have, with my fire place so sweet. My sofa and chair with a recliner for my feet, and all the trimmings that will make this room complete.

And Oh! Yes my kitchen such a beautiful sight. An Island so sweet with chairs to sit and eat. A refrigerator and stove, such a blessing to behold. A clock and what knots, I thank you Lord for all I've got.

My dinning room so sweet, with table and chairs for eight to eat, with decorations on the wall, a beautiful site for all, A China Cabinet will make this room complete for me and my husband to be.

LaVerne W. Henson

My office is a blessing from you Lord. My computer and desk, and other little things like books, pens and paper, I am so grateful. My paintings on the wall and such, you have blessed me with so much. And a special thanks for my Copier and Fax. Thank you Lord for bringing me back to a better home. where I can relax.

My exercise room is a dream come true, thank you Lord for all that you will do, so I can keep in shape that I may relate, and not be sluggish and out of shape. Thank you Lord for this room so neat, and all the necessary equipment you will bless me to complete.

My bathroom is beautiful and fair it has a chair and vanity there. A spacious tub, a separate shower with a connection hose, a large closet with plenty room to hang my clothes, my shoes and all the things that I may choose.

Thank you Lord for my bedroom suit with night stand dresser and chest. Oh! I thank you Lord you have blessed. A bed so cozy and sweet soon to have and to hold my husband will be complete.

HAPPY BIRTHDAY

Today is your birthday, a beautiful day it is. To see your smiling face, how grand it is to live. Today is your birthday, the beginning of many more. To receive best wishes, presents and gifts from shore to shore.

Today is your birthday, a pleasant time indeed. To be of service to you and cater to your needs. Today is your birthday, given from above, Jesus is the reason, you have lived for many seasons.

Happy, Happy Birthday and many blessings too, may God bless you the whole year through.

GOD OF ALL SEASONS

Thank you Lord for the seasons. We thank you Lord for many reasons.

We thank you for the food we eat, clothes we wear, our homes, cars, our jobs so rare, and all our blessings that's in your care.

Thank you Lord for the seasons. We thank you Lord for many reasons.

To share with our family and friends, gifts from far and near, and all our Christmas cheer throughout the year. You have blessed us with all seasons, Spring, Summer, Winter and Fall, you are the God of all.

Thank you Lord for the seasons. We thank you Lord for many reasons.

Thank you Lord for all you have done. Thank you Lord most of all for sacrificing your only Son, who paid the price with his life, that we might have the right to the Tree of Life.

GIVING THANKS

These are some of my answered prayers, thank you Lord for being there.
In 1997 I lost my home on Baraboo Drive, and for three years the Lord led me from place to place seeking shelter from here and there, from friends and relatives everywhere.

After three years of struggling the Lord blessed me with this job at the Auto Pound in March of 2000, to take me off the street, that I may have food to eat, shelter from the cold and heat, a place to lay my head that I may rest in my own bed.

After working one month, the Lord blessed me to find my own apartment on Duncanville Road, so cozy and sweet that's close to my job and even closer to the Church I attend each week. The Buss stops running after ten, but the Lord bless me any way to make it in.

After working nine months at the Auto Pound, I was pressed in my spirit to go buy a car in 12/2000. It was on a cold winters day with snow on the ground, when I had no way of getting around. But the Lord blessed, he made a way, my neighbor drove me, and he was very kind to me that day. And the same day I drove home with my 1996 Mist. Thank you Lord, the car you gave me to drive and so, it takes me every where I need to go.

After a few years, the Lord blessed me to pay my car off with out stress. Thank you Lord you are the best. He didn't stop there he blessed me with another Home all my own, where I am to day, thank you Lord for bringing me this way.

LaVerne W. Henson

My 1996 Mist. Gave me trouble after 10 years. Thank you Lord for making a way that I may have a new car this day. My New Ford made my life comfortable and secure thank you Lord for being there.

Thank you Lord for the things I learned on the way, I will always be thankful you led me that way. You restored all I lost, even more and better, thank you Lord you are my God in heaven.

JUST A LITTLE THOUGHT

This little thought was very sudden and unplanned, but never the less we will miss your smiling face, and every thing you usually put in place. I didn't get to know you very well. But what I can tell, I really believe you are swell.

Everyone is going out of their way to let you know we will miss you when you go. So don't forget to come by and say hello. Whatever the situation, whatever the cause, Just remember, it's a reason why you were called. This entire shift wish you well, we know you can handle whatever the job entails.

THE KING

The Virgin Mary was to be the espoused wife of Joseph; but before they came together, it was declared in the heavens A Virgin shall be with child and bring forth a son conceived of the Holy One, and His name shall be called Emanuel, the Savior of our souls from all the sin we hold.

There were wise men that came to see that which was born for you and me. They saw His star in the East, even they had to come and worship the King of Peace. The Wise Men presented him with gifts of gold, frankincense and myrrh and bowed to honor the greatest King on earth.

We celebrate this great advent, not just in the season do we resound this voice. But to understand that today and every day there's a reason to rejoice. This Mighty God who humbled Himself for the entire world to see, became a servant in the fashion of man, just to save sinners like you and me

Jesus is called Wonderful, Counselor, The Mighty God, The Everlasting Father, and The Prince of Peace. His Kingdom rules over land and sea, and whatever we need him for, He'll be there for you and me. So let every heart prepare Him room, let heaven and nature sing for the Lord is come and He's brought joy to the world.

LET EARTH RECEIVE HER KING